Blackberries

Volume 3, Collected Poems

Burton L. Carlson

Bloomington, IN

Milton Keynes, UK

AuthorHouse™
1663 Liberty Drive, Suite 200
Bloomington, IN 47403
www.authorhouse.com
Phone: 1-800-839-8640

AuthorHouse™ UK Ltd.
500 Avebury Boulevard
Central Milton Keynes, MK9 2BE
www.authorhouse.co.uk
Phone: 08001974150

First published by AuthorHouse 2/12/2007

ISBN: 978-1-4259-8267-6 (sc)

Printed in the United States of America
Bloomington, Indiana

This book is printed on acid-free paper.

→ Volume 3 ←

Contents

PART I

PART II

PART III

Part I

Blackberries

Packed in this segmented fruit is a kind of truth
peculiar to jellies and jams
and to the times
I ran through Oregon weather,
unleashed, in rain.

In those days, I believed in resurrection.

It was first when
we came back for a visit to the coast,
when you were just showing with our only child,
that I saw again
the sawmill village of my youth.

It was not the same,

and today I find myself asking
if we ever shared
enough parts of our fragmented lives
to assure a wine
dry and full as the blackberry wine
that we drank that day.

I find blackberries here in the store.
They don't ship well
and I'm forced to make do with the frozen.
Still they make good pies
and the truth drips to burn in the oven.

I extend my days from one berry season to the next.
I do not put store
in the promise of life after death.
I have tried that twice.

My life will contribute its flavor
when the fruit is ripe.

Emulating Hymenoptera (For Donald W. Baker)

1.

The poems I find most touching are the ones
that brush the skin of childhood, graze the cones
that once were filled with syrup, browse the sacks
that once stored bursts of popcorn.
There the salt
of butter, still attractive, and the melt
of ice cream, cotton candy, colored snow
invite quick wings and buzzing.
Fragile bees
and wasps and yellow-jackets search out sweets
where fairground gates are locked and hornets treat
themselves to beads of loss that once were sweat.
What's left is what most matters.
Think of seeds,
as if a poem like this one could be grown
and tongued off sticky paper. Take this room.
The bed is someone else's, rain has blown
and sun has bleached the covers.
What I own
are fingers on the keyboard. Keyboards click
and make the sound of insects. Words, like bees,
scout out the hidden meadows, hollow trees,
that compass in my life.
Keys dance them home.

2.

The paper nests of hornets,
spit by spit,
accumulate to houses, nurseries hid
and shingled, many layered,
row on row.
The larvae
in their casings
swell to burst.

I think of rain and bullets
and the sound that paper makes when tearing.
Warring bees
like rain
attack the window.
Foolish wrens
have broken necks this way
or fallen stunned.

Still poems preserve a sweetness.
I have come
to seek the taste of flowers.
On my tongue are marigold
and bee balm.
There are poems that I will never write
as there are rooms
that I will never enter.
Still the sum
must be a sum of sweetness.

Reedy lives
of summer vibrate down,
but perfume clings
and fingers go on clicking,
simple fare
this time
of ink and paper.
Winter bears
translucent in the sun
tear open hives.

3.

My hunger
is transparent
scouting trees
that drip with sweetness,

trees
that proffer cones,
the salt of which
is resin.

Right or wrong,
it's been
hard work
to knock
the old nests
down
and every
year
rebuild
them.

There's
no home
more solidly connected,
tighter tied
to rafters
than
these nests
and I am glad
to let
wind have them,

wind
that like a bee
is never
constant,
settles,
                then is gone.

4.

And so
I cre
dit bees,
present
them
gifts

and catch
them in
my hands
to let
them go
like flow
ers cast
on wa
ters,
liv
ing bread
that will
one day
bring pro
fit. You have said
that pa
tience is
what counts.
I coun
ter: bees
and wasps
and yel
low jac
kets. Such as these,
if childish in
beginning,
swarm to grow
and congregate to visions,
over
flow,
like
drip
pings
from
a
fau
cet,
sweets and stings.

5.

I struggle to beginnings.

Still the child
that was and never was,
but lived to grow and grew to age,
now aged,
declines to die,

revisits lost beginnings,
seeks out hives,
abandoned nests, dead lanterns, hollow trees,
and shredded paper sacks.

An old man's poem,
like summer-scented beeswax,
stores up sun
and pollen for transference.
Young mouths feed
on love once made abundant,
then was lost.

Blackbird

1. Goodbye

Blackbirds make public their notice.

Across the sky in flocks as thick as cloud
they say goodbye,

and it's winter as simple as that.

2. Cousins

Blackbirds and grackles, glad cousins,
amass in fields
like dark congregations
for corn
or, again, in trees
come together to gossip and fidget.

3. Explosion

I have seen birds primed
to explode into air by the thousands,

swirl about like leaves,

curl down like tornadoes
into trees,

there to swarm like bees

and await trigger happy
the shout

that ignites release.

4. Hello

I think of myself as a blackbird.
I don't know why.

There are times, I suppose, when goodbye
is the best word said.

There are times when hello is appropriate.

I lie in bed and whistle to myself
Bye, Bye, Blackbird.

5. Trolling

Each year birds trawl,
hauling nets once in spring,
once in fall,
and with each pass pull
a train of collective anarchy.

They arrive in shifts
like workers let out from a factory
or perhaps like ships
conveyed on the ocean,
riding swells.

6. Politics

In the fall, it's talk,
all strut about confabulation.

With quips they fly:

these tribes,

these equivocal councils,

this unformed nation.

Dogwoods (For Liz)

Finally I am measuring your death
who have never cried,
not even been able to get angry.
Oh, I have tried
and admit to being depressed.

Dogwoods, I guess,
have brought me to this pass in the spring
when like girls they seem
to flicker in and out
among trees.

I can see your knees
just showing beneath your white dress
and the way you tied
your hair
with a ribbon that was pink.

Who will decide
if it's you or the dogwoods I mourn
on this April morning
when children are loud in the sun
and the green grass shines
almost white
in the health of its innocence?

I expect your feet
and the sounds of your voice
and your laughter.
It would not surprise,
not even these fifteen years after.

I take delight
in how fragile still are these trees
and the timid knees
of little girls
dressed up for Easter.

Doors

Finality is no friend to decision.

I like best doors
that perpetually hang just ajar,
that a cat can swing
or the wind slam shut
in the night
with the windows up.

There should never be a lock put on doors.
If there's expression
to locks
and to doors without swing,
I would say depression
and hours of unrelieved sleep
are the signs to watch.

Doors are meant to be hinged,
tinged with exit.

Unlike a wall,
doors are never quite sure,
not explicit,
can be made to swing
by the youngest the furthest
without thought.

It's the nearest thing to forgiveness
and perhaps to love
to leave the screen door unhooked
and the door latch open.

Fledging

1. Robins

Three sets of robins fledged and so did love
fly off, well fed,
a second time and third.
The naked bird
that stirs within the nest
and must be fed with every worm and pest
soon learns to fly
and, fledged, is born once more,
this time to death
and to life's full repertoire.

2. Marriage

We sought to match our efforts to the claims
for food and trust and caring.
We were good,
but never good enough.

The robe I'm wearing
is what my father wore,
the very same.

I sit now at my window
first to claim
returning birds, remembering their calls.

I do enjoy the sun.

Sun warms my blood
and brings back summer mornings
when the doves
in numbers far too dense
fed on the lawn
and carried on love making.

Like the doves, I go to bed quite early.

I am told love should no longer matter,
but it does.

Confession

The lines of geese are noisy,
belling dogs.

My small dog stops,
cocks ears,
does not look up.

The hawks and owls
have never been a threat.

Instead, the howls
of police car and ambulance
arrest her.

She turns and tucks
her tail to sit and answer.

Then her wail
that makes my hair stand up
like Job joins in
the feral group confession
of her kin.

Days Of Passing (For Elizabeth)

These days are days of passing. All day long
I hear the flights of geese conducting south.

You're heading north to Medford. It is tough
to know I can't protect. You're on your own.

Which is as it should be. But all the same
your empty room means I am moving on

to my own kind of school and toward the rest
that I have earned while you have just begun.

It makes me know that I shall never know
the beauty you'll accomplish, not in whole.

I know some parts already and am proud.
And so it is with pride I let you go

to what it is awaits, to your own place
and wish you all the best. Not much for prayers,

I wish for you good love and much success
and not a lot of sickness, pain or death

among the ones you love. I will move on
and that is how it is. You should take joy

from all the joy you've brought, with luck confront
the things I didn't do and should have done

and things I did that you would never know
but someday may bring thanks. So I pass on

to southward like the geese and other birds.
These sounds are yours to keep and build upon.

Leaves

1. Raking

The leaves fall to the ground like used up days.
My daughter runs to catch them.
One by one, they flee her reaching hands
but are contained, retrieved by rakes to piles.

The leaf piles stand as temporary mountains she and friends
are avid to destroy and do succeed
in part
before sharp voices start them home.

Then I move in to bundle.

What for me are testaments to loss, some smooth, some frayed,
once pressed in bags surprise me:
just how large
in volume and in weight these thin texts are
that once brought shade and comfort.

Now the yard is silent as a church and as remote.
Stars shine through clashing branches.
Voices call from rooms where light is warm
and food awaits,

but I am not yet ready,
have not crossed the necessary t's, put dots to i's,
or signed my name in ink
and placed a date
among the shifting branches on this page
so brightly filled with stars.

I cannot think these minutes make a difference,
add or mar.

2. Space

It is a jagged night.

A racking wind has battered plastic remnants,
sent stained sheets of newsprint to the corners.

Salmon seek out streams where they were spawned;
likewise tonight my thoughts are crowding back,
my feet so cold they could be sunk in mud.

My cold nose runs.
I hawk and spit clear liquid.

Still, at peace,
I track the blue-black heavens in their sweep
as long as I can stand it,
fingers numb in gloves and ears like ice.

Where we come from,
perhaps where we will go,
is blank black space,
billions of years of nothing.

Then came grace that warmed us like a smile,
that made this place for all we know
the only one called home among the starry billions:

our own sun.

3. Herding

There's a shiver born of cold and wind swept chasms
that spasms the intestines, that draws in
the testicles and penis.

Muscles hoard the body's flow of sap,
its sugared blood.

The breath I breathe is white,
as is the smoke that scatters from the chimneys pale as chalk.
The clouds are flocks of sheep that got left out.

The starry slate of heaven is a slope on which dogs I imagine
    spin and race
like demons full of teeth that drop to pace
heads low, intent to whistles, creeping, slow,
then up again to nip at erring heels
or circle back, flat out, the way they've come to lie at last,
work done,
and hang tongues out.

My mind crowds in on thoughts like errant sheep and drives
    them to conclusion,
not so much by force or by confusion, but relief.
The cold has worn me down.

I let the wind that gathers bear me home like so much grief.

I open up the door, bring chill air in,
step in to warmth of voice and warm hands' touch.

Dancing Lessons

1. Hunger

What it comes of is hunger or sickness,
two points of view,
this need of a body to touch, to lock and move
in rhythm with a another body,

clock thigh on thigh, spread fingers of one hand on the back
and with pressure guide
the direction and the placement of feet;

when the music rests,
let go without merriment or loss,
give the hand a shake,
and move on to another encounter, another face

that in hair style and motion is different,
or in strength and grace
invites adjustment and response;

so reduce the space
and sway like an elm tree in place,
causing joy to climb the exuberant curve of raw muscle
in a race with time.

2. Resolution

For too much of my life
I've looked back.

I turn to face
your arms that require
a tension.

You invite weight
and balance that weight
with your own.

My feet and legs
you ticket
in the way they should go.

You compel my arms
to form a firm rail
you can lean on.

We walk through steps
so I can inspect
all the flavors,

a child explore
the storewide varieties
of touch,

perfume you wear,
until all I hear
is your music.

My thoughts speed up.
I anticipate
the end of the dance

and the hope to dance it
more than once
as we transit the floor,

weighing risks and chances.

3. Connection

So, yes, hold me close for this moment and for each you can,
stand swaying for a time without music in a dance that feels
reliable and trusting as a friend as our old bones creak
and cast off the Mondays and Tuesdays, the endless weeks
of weariness and abstinence and loss, and sometimes speak
to each other from a distance on the phone until alone,
once again we stand holding each other, my penis grown
against the softness of your belly, your candy tongue
sharp and strawberry sweet in my mouth as we climb the rungs
together of anticipation and together come
to the end of the dance, being mortal, and the cold walk home.

4. Refuge

And so fulfill expectation.

And so you time your movements and moods to my own.
You do not decline
my wish to rub my face in your hair.

What we need as our muscles decline
is a gentle stair
to a room where the bedclothes are aired
with the sun at noon;

a place where, itself, time is kind
and erases worry
up close when the lighting is dim.

Which is why we come
without words to our pillows and our bed
and the safety net that was altar and refuge
for our lives,

where we offered sweat
and tears and the mingling of ourselves,
not without regret,
also gladly and accompanied by laughter.

The wine came after
and was red as the sun to our eyes.

5. Freedom

Soon bleached and worn,
we will spoon our two bodies together and wait for sleep.
(like sheep, we can hear people say, like complacent sheep)
still expecting to wake up together,
two birds at dawn,
and lie, blankets drawn, hand-in-hand
to discuss the weather and health,
and anything else whatsoever
all in good time.

Concavities, Pock Marks, Depression

1.

Depressions relate to the weather.

Pock marks can be
the wear made by war on a wall.

Sometimes despair
we describe as the suck of a hole.

The things we share,
when gathered together, have depth.

New graves make clear
how lightly what we gather adheres

and how absurd
are the things we had hoped
might have happened.

2.

As we grow old,
time leads in a different direction.

We give or hold,
remember or ignore what we're told.

The holes that serve
in the alley are rounded and shallow,
in all ways spare.

These dust baths created by sparrows
cause me to smile,

as do cones that an ant lion hollows,

and the way dark soil
slides up and away from the share,

as if all toil
is relatively unimportant.

3.

It's amazing how
little depends on our digging;

how our digging tends
toward whatever we thought not to know;

how raw truth bends
and twists in pursuit of its meaning;

how grid and trench
are meant to sift fact after screening;

how in the end,
very little that we know is put right,

but is like a song
the words of which are not found,

but are not forgotten.

Truth Saying

1.

I am a man who sits, but once was young,
heart porous as an apple.
I am become the shadow of my father.

My own son will never be my shadow.
Perhaps that's good.

My son who took his life won't have to look
at my life
like the book his life forsook.

Perhaps my son was anxious to undo
a deed he'd done
or stop himself from doing what he feared.

The tears at least are past.
It will take years and lives beyond my death
to put at rest the questions and the doubts.

But what of debts?

I ask myself once more what makes men strong,
why some men choose to fail,
choose to be wrong;

or why persistent torment drives those down
who bow their knee
and ask forgiveness from
the wives and mothers driven to reform,

so make of love a gauntlet: smile or frown.

2.

My only son and father, both of whom
knew love could lead to slaughter,
too, were sons
who chose against their fathers; still refused
to be the men
they knew themselves to be.

The truth is I'm ashamed of my own need
to find some saving virtue,
ease the hurt
of lives the pain of which leaves only scars;

admit at last my simple need to come
hand out, as would a beggar,
to receive,
instead of coins, a blessing;

to retrieve
from ashes and lost hopes and self-deceit
the truth that joins all men
at final rout:

the joy we knew as boys
before came doubts.

→ Part II ←

For Corydon James Carlson, 1965 – 1997

Sitting With The Dead, Hartford Hospital (First Attempt, 1997)

Prologue

We practice the first time by leaning,
pull up to stand
and reach out,
reach out
with one hand,
hang on with the other.

My son, my brother,
has reached out to death as to a mother,
but did not let go.
Almost,
almost,
but not quite.

I hold his hand.
Once again, he take steps.
I am the father.
I will not let go.
Not quite,
not quite,
until he says so.

1. Emergency

When I got the call,
it was headlights and taillights
eight hours.

Now, I see breath rise,
rise and fall, rise and fall
under sheets,
see the thin knees bend,
lift sheets like a mountain,
raise a tent,
drop and let sheets
fall.

My mind is far off,
touching fields,
not the Jayhawk ranks
that rise by the road eight feet tall,
but the winter stubble,
Indiana cut back to pale rubble,

straw ends that guide
our eyes in a squint to the sun
along lines that run
as if ruled
to that point in the snow
where all lines converge.

2. Winter

I loved to walk harvested fields, lands ploughed or fallow,
climb fences, build a fire, warm my hands,
walk my own tracks home
in a jacket with the collar turned up
against wind that followed.

It was usually on Sunday after church
with both parents home
that I sought out the solace of the fields,
leaving talk and meals to walk the blank whiteness alone,

loving winter cold
and the "haves" and "have nots" that go with it,
livestock in barns
and cornstalks stacked up in bare fields
like the shocks of arms
you see in old Civil War photos.

What a cornfield brings
is the grace to let winter winds blow,
let the dead crops go to get on with what living is left,
let the drifting snow
cover knowledge and patterns of before,
let the wind and drifts
prepare for the living that will come.

3. Intermission

And so my son, who reminds me so much of my father,
lies there in bed
and I feel once again need to talk,
to together walk and share things we never have said.

What he says is this: just how easy it is, just a step,
just a simple step,
one step, then a second, then one
and the end has come before you can know
or regret it.

He's not glad he failed.
He knows he was foolish to try.
He accepts the price his body and the doctors demand.
It's a whole new hand,
these cards he has drawn and must play.

He has learned that hell is something no man can avoid,
that the same slack well that refreshes
can suck a man down,
even when he's drowned
can force him to vomit his guts.

Epilogue

I look with pride
on this son who has failed
and survived,
welcome home the man
that with this single act
he becomes.

I am not afraid
of either the road
he has walked
or the stakes he's played.
I am rocking myself
as he sleeps.

I make up a song
as I did
when he was a child.
I was young then
and could hold him
and would rock him to sleep,

just a nonsense song
I'll remember and sing to myself
and will repeat
like a prayer or a mantra
or beads.

It is what I need.
Maybe someone is there
who can hear
and knows how to listen..

Imperfect Grass (Breckenridge, August 1998)

And so on his grandfather's birthday,
he killed himself,
not thinking, I suppose, that it mattered,
that perhaps the date had nothing to do with his action,
that it was too late,
in any case,
to work up the traction it would take to stop.

Or, perhaps, with some logic he thought
he would find him there in light at the end of the tunnel,
his arms spread out in greeting and anticipation,
with a sudden shout having left what it was he was doing,
put a jacket on,
and rushed out to meet as to a train.

In this way the brain deals with grief and with anger and with loss.
There is so much pain that emotion itself gets spread out
like a blot in rain
or a blanket of mud behind the eyes.
What is left is strain.
It is difficult even to remember.
Still I know that time will pass and a flatness take over.

Alone I climb up high where wild grasses are growing
and pikas line
rocky tunnels with their winter hay.
Here air is thin and my breathing is labored and rapid.
Here I begin
my count of things fragile that pass:
dry grass that burns
for a short time, but gives sudden light.

The Climber (Or Humpty-Dumpty)

The wall he fell down was not steep, but the fall was far
beyond where a father could reach.

Like a falling star,
no more could he unbend in an instant what the hand of time
closed fingers on and claimed for its own.

He could not out climb his own sense of guilt.
Failing purpose, his legs too numb
and his breathing too harsh,
he lost purchase.

It was not much fun.

Alone and in pain, he lay down.
It was now his wish to forget, to be free, and to sleep.
Sleep would be a balm in a world that had tortured too long.
It would be a test
to see if at last he could rest.

Now his breath was calm.
He no longer thought of struggle and pain.
Peace was like a song that only he was able to sing

and it fell like rain.

Mouse

These days are days of sameness,
mountains flat and waves without emotion.

Time moves on, but I cannot remember names of days
and would not know the time except the sun
begins its route each morning.

Thought shuts down to grayness, plain and simple,
like a mouse,
now flat and desiccated in a trap,
that once was filled with life and ran about
and squeezed through cracks too thin
and got lost in an open box of cereal.

Where I tossed the box the mouse was in is just out back
where birds are fat with pleasure
and the cat
that is my neighbor's cat renews her hunt.

Lost Child

1. Suicide

Perhaps it came from falling up the sky.
If so, it wasn't falling,
but a reach
for life and space for breathing.
Like a plant,
he stretched his hand to light.
His grasp fell short.

Or there's perhaps a story
we don't know
that caused his mind to wobble out of plumb
and spin for breathless moments
until drums
of waiver and imbalance
drove him down.

So much we'll never know,
and so repeat guessed reasons,
useless questions,
trace his climb from nothing back to nothing,
sit to breathe
and when recovered rise,
like time move on.

2. Preparation

The lost child is a wound that does not close,
that seeps and never fills.

Flesh does not heal,
anneals perhaps a while,
still love leaks out.

The emptiness,
another name for grief
and time's untimely temper,
builds up slow
like leaves or snow in winter,

wiping tracks.

There is no more reprieve,
no going back, no argument to try, no untried tack.

There is no lack of truth.

Death is a fact.

3. The Funeral

The sole surviving children still rely
on strength of hand and eye to make things right.

They are, at once, the living and take care,
at least for now, of parents, drinks, and chairs.

Each child grows older faster. This, they think,
is what it means to love: your options shrink.

4. The Wish

And as for me, I dwindle.
Flesh grows small
and appetite has failed.

I could have shared.

Perhaps he thought I'd argue;
or was scared
and did not dare to think.

The latter is more likely.

He was closed
and focused on himself.
He couldn't see beyond his need
the hurt.

His shirt unclean, he couldn't ask for love.

I understand.

But still I wish I could have held
his hand.

5. Afterwards

And so I sit with poems.

The private grief
that poems like this make public
is a grief
that looks at life directly,
leaves us stunned
like cattle
axed
before our throats are cut.

It's not the death,
but death that's willed that stops me,
so much pain
that life becomes the death
that death sets free.

How do I understand?

It seems I don't.

And still I go on trying,
come to rest,
if ever, with the snow,

the holy snow that covers and is cold,
but also warms
where cold is so much deeper.

Like the arms
of mothers, wives, and lovers
snow is blessed
and given as a blessing one last task:

to hold within the cold what warmth is left.

6. Acceptance

And so relive experience,
wrapped in snow
and fog as in a cover,
what we know
blanked out
and unfamiliar.

Drifts that grow
soon overtop the fence.
Converging rows
of stubble
stretch no longer.

Strength is spent
and what is left is hunger,
sleet or snow,
the hoarfrost on a branch,
the ridge that blows
the ghost of snow like smoke.

Without the cold
there is no need for fire.
Fences grow
of post and board
or wire,
but it's snow
that sets its own accords,
absorbs the sun
and seeks new life as water,
drips and flows.

Storm

Depression comes in summer like a storm
that sweeps in unexpected,
building clouds that turn a day to night.

Deep darkness forms.

The next thing, lights go out.
You hear hail knock and think of crops and loss.

If you look out, you see the shape of trees
and how limbs toss, you think, like limbs in hell.

It's just as well you have no eye for color.

Absent news, the house becomes a prison, faces shut
and white almost to death.

But these storms pass.

You see the track in limbs and wires down,
perhaps a treelike dragon on its back,

and wait for birds to sing.

The birds storms drown, in any case, are few.

Most birds survive and with each bird a song.
It would be wrong to think that birds won't sing.

It's what birds do.

Inside The Mountain

To live inside the mountain takes more care.
There's darkness, always darkness.

Stairs are there, precipitous and steep, and places where
the stairs fall clean away.

Sometimes the heat built up in ancient fissures causes steam
and seams of coal to burn.

It takes more grace than earnings, faith than works, to damp
  coal down.

And sometimes dig out gold and precious gems to bring up
  to the surface,
sewn in hems, unpolished and uncut,
a thing we do to move beyond the boredom,
store up hope.

Or sit sometimes in darkness, absent dew,
beside dark flowing rivers,
sit to smoke and listen to the silence, earth's stark prayer,
and presuppose the answer.

There's the clink and clunk of blunt machines,
the dull drill's roar resounding in the walls
and, almost sore,
the strain on lungs to breathe.

Down here the score is always none to ten.
We find that more is something less than less.
There is the stress
of halls like hulls of ships we pump to drain.

The simple lack of light makes sense of smell
and touch of more importance.
Here the ear can feel as much as hear what we should know.

We're bound by life to listen.

It is well to notice walls that tremble, air that glows,
direction to the exit
and the slow pay out of breath like candy:
buy or sell.

But more important, darkness
and the fear it gathers to itself
and so preserves
creation like a book left on a shelf,
the pages still uncut, the binding sealed.

It is by trust we're healed,
by blindness cope down deep inside earth's crust,
here where the care of hope is simple habit:
that and prayer.

Last Word

Renewal comes from sorrow, not from grief,
and grief is deferential, wends its way
the way a word repeats, the way a theme
comes back again in music or a tongue
returns to touch once more the aching gum.

That is the way with grief. It overcomes
by simple repetition, wears us down
and is worn out, not lost. Grief slowly yields,
becomes a part of background. Grief backs down,
but never goes away.

Grief is unwound
like springs inside a clock. Grief hangs around,
a son's unwanted friend, a daughter's choice,
a voice no longer pressing. Grief is dumb
and, as such, is compelling; stands in line
and breaks the whole to parts while touching none.

We say grief is an orphan, has no home,
but houses in the heart. And grief repeats,
repeats and then repeats. It strings its beads
of onyx on a chain to stake its claim
to thoughtless repetition.
Grief retreats
in mirrors facing mirrors. What grief tests
is love and if love lasts. It's love and grief
locked in domestic battle. Which outlasts
is hard to say: love grapples, grief holds on.
And so they sway as one,
this way and that.

→ Part III ←

Weight Of Water

1.

The shifting weight of water, so like silk,
slides down what it contains. It builds and spills
like lingerie down legs to puddle floors.
It fits because it fills. There is no tuck
that brings bath water closer. Water sucks
its way up stems and hills. It has a will
to fill gaps left to fill. It drives the truck
of steam that turns the turbine and the wheels
that, flooded, force the paddles.
                                        Water yields.
It cools and toils like Job, lifts up or roils
and gives away its power, slick as oil.
It falls as silent snow or copies speech,
makes laughter as it trickles. Water flows,
yet, water is a constant and defines
the dryness we call desert. Water rhymes
with what we use to dry it or it chimes
the steps of time with drips.
                                        Direct to God
we rise from cleansing water, newly scrubbed
and rinsed of sin like mud, still all the lust
we put back on with pockets weighs us down.
We wonder at the whales that do not drown
down where the mountains rest in dark and cold.
The pressure is enormous. We grow old.
Compressed to what we are, not one bone straight,
we feel our way to stories. Shedding weight,
we push to darkness, sounding. We count down
to roots we can't imagine and the song
that whales sing, like an echo, threads our blood.

2.

The weight of water fools us, bearing down
when we had thought, like rain, it would run off
to fill an empty aquifer or drop
to mutter in a cistern, free of salts
and used to wash girls' hair. It does appear,
more often than expected, heaven pours
a burst of cloud upon us, giving more
than we had hoped or wished for. Worse is drought
that turns the faucet handle inside out
and sucks out all emotion -- love and guilt
and anger, fear and sadness. Sometimes pain
provokes a brand of desert where the wind
fills every pore with dust until a rain,
miles off, fills rims brim full and drives a wall
of mud to suffocate or flood to stall.

And sometimes water freezes and we think
it's safe to walk upon, but cracks begin
and we are left to swim in cold or drown
down deep among the fish. Water is round
or square or deep or shallow. Water takes
the shape we choose to give it, even fakes
its presence as a lake when there is not
a drop of water near. Still water bears
more often tons than pounds. If water slays,
it's weight at work, not malice. Or it shrinks
like hemorrhoids and purpose. Water fills
the chinks that purpose leaves and quickly chills
the heat of sex, the fever that is gold.

3.

The gentle hand of water wears us down
and smoothes us like a stone. It is the lens
that changes our perspective, bends the lines
of vision and perception, makes our aim
a measured calculation if we care
or hit-and-miss assumption if we don't.
Still water carries back, transports the pain
that gives life its compunction, rising up,
providing current when our sails are shut.

Fast water covers sound, and if we cut
a hand, it is in water that we plunge,
as plunge we do when weather is too hot
or insects bite, or playing hide-and-seek
we seek to hide our footprints or, if not,
then misdirect attention.
                                        Dowsers swear
it's water that we're made of, that ascribes
the limit to intent and where we walk.
Or water copies waking, wipes us blank.
Yet, water is correction, is the link
that carries with it silt, adds weight to milk
and fills the breast to feed us.

                                        Water winks
as moisture in the eye and shines on teeth,
emerges from our pores as sweat and shrinks
our shirts with armpit wetness. If we fear,
it is our palms we wipe and then our tears,
as if hands had a choice. Add water's voice,
heard first before our birth, and mouths go dry:
no tear to weep, no spittle to rejoice.

4.

Or violently attacks us, body slams
that leave us dead or damaged, work of waves
and floods and savage currents where what's saved
is shredded, if we're lucky. Water's tough,
or will be if we let it, pushes, shoves,
is macho in its way, then pulling back,
reverses flow and currents, treasures love
in quiet backward eddies, slowing time.
Or water hits the limit, drives the tide
that circumscribes extension, marks the curve
that cells aspire to, together serve
in sequence, not eternal, here and gone,
but every time replaced.
                                                            The water song
that whales sing, that my body, not as strong
as once it was when young, can also hum
and move to when I move my feet along
the sidewalks in my town and cannot sleep.
And sing, too, when I wake and push my feet
in jeans I haven't fastened, lift the seat
and spit before I piss, take self in hand
and shake what drops are left, then zip my pants
and sit to tie my shoes.
                                                            My morning walks,
like checkers, chess or horseshoes, post a score
I share with wife and doctor, then again
like Ahab walk the deck, tie up loose ends
before the night arrives and darkness bends
trees, rocks, and glass to purpose. There's no need,
as once, to set alarms before I sleep.

5.

I am a child of water, drip and spout,
the cells that fill my skin, the womb from out
of which I swam, a fish. It's what I am:
a wieldy weight of water held by dams
and sometimes arms that hold.

If I look back,
I'm caught inside a falls, a tidal wave
convincing as Niagara. Life spills out
and overflows its pitcher, pouring doubt
like foam that's raised on milk and spreading guilt
to make a mess that mops can never dry.
We see and hear what current offers up
of what we once cast forth.

And so I lean,
my footing less than solid, what I mean
not always what I say and what I do,
not always my intent. The parent streams
of other lives converge. I swim or fend
and in the end sink down or wash ashore,
another raft of flotsam, something more
for scavengers to gather, burn or carve.

And yet I want to think life's water's pure
to swallow and to bathe in like the birds
that bathe on streets in puddles. Or it seems
that water drives emotion, dictates dreams
and acts beyond compulsion, pushes need
beyond what senses touch. It's not enough
that I should sit and listen, kiss and suck
and pinch and bite and lick. I must stand up
and reach back, pull and lift, resist the tide.

6.

There's miles to go, I know, and miles behind.

I'm mesmerized by streetlights, see the blur
that comes from hours of swimming, know this light
is but my haloed vision. I have drowned,
at least the boy I was, but not the thirst
that follows night time swimming or, reversed,
begins each day with coffee, juice and milk.

I think myself reluctant, but I'm not,
not even on my worst days. I betray
what's clearly in my interest and give up
the secrets that I love and give away
what gives me my identity: I flood.

Tears, fear and shame come easy. It's a mood
that strikes like summer lightning, blows like rain
on Hoosier afternoons and pulls a train
of memory in its wake, the lovely smell
of earth and grass and moisture and the swell
of breasts in rain wet shirts and hard prick's strain,
emotions I remember.
Still, it's plain
that when rain finally stops and curbs take up
from streets that day's collection, streams run off,
first find their way to gutters, then to drains,
I'm thankful for my body, pipes that work,
the conduits, tubes and channels still unblocked
and viaducts that carry lymph and blood,
the waste and sweat and urine given off
by pleasure and by habit.
Up above,
the moisture that I breathe collects to clouds.

7.

The fact is, water chastens. I can't save
reflections from a stream, the flash of waves
confronted by the sun as water makes
its own iambic statement, mapping back
and back and back and back, a lapping sound
with minor variations. Rain and streams
and rivers, lakes and oceans move as one,
as my poems sound as one, as all my life
experiences, remembered, add to one,
repeating and hypnotic.
                                        Whales begin
the moan of their myopic hymns alone
and sing first to themselves. The sound resounds,
a modulated whistle, shore to shore
as buoys take up the echo. Songs I sing
are also to myself. They're what I bring
from each long day's exhaustion, joy and grief.
The singing comes as blessing.
                                        The relief
that comes to heart with singing and is shunned
by those who do not sing is also one
that can be touched and handled, any chord
that thumb and little finger stretched can reach,
or one hand held can pour, the something more
that water in its mercy flows to teach:
the play of time and water where a beach
confronts the wear of waves and is not breached
by castles that I build or words I rhyme.

8.

The last drips are the slowest.

Last drips pause
to catch the last reflection.

Then they drop.

Printed in the United States
71270LV00006B/249

9 781425 982676